Retirement Rescue:

Seven Lessons to Save Your Retirement

Dan Cuprill & Nikki Earley

Preface

For over twenty years, our firm has conducted retirement planning seminars for people who are sick of work and ready to make a major change in their life. It can be a rather stressful time, for mistakes made at this station are often irrevocable.

Much of what you'll read in the pages ahead comes from the messages we deliver in those seminars.

For the sake of good writing, we use masculine pronouns to describe people (as opposed to the more politically correct "he or she." As you'll soon discover, we try to remember what our teachers taught us.

This book is a personal finance book like no other: it contains very few numbers. Lord knows we have plenty of books that do, and we're not smart enough to improve on them. This book is also rather short for two reasons. One, we're lazy; and two, the message is a fairly simple one (especially when you accept that unless you own a time traveling DeLorean like Marty McFly in *Back to the Future*, the future is not predictable).

We will describe many of the quantitative aspects of personal finance, but the biggest obstacle to investor success remains the investor himself. We are human, and as humans, we are naturally wired to eschew pain. We seek pleasure when we can, but the absence of pain is paramount.

It is this "survival mechanism" that kept early cave dwellers motivated to stay warm, find food, and avoid sabretooth tigers. Today, it keeps us fat, avoiding exercise (which for many is painful), and eating fast food (which is pleasurable), while contracting diabetes and hypertension along the way.

The survival mechanism has also caused the average investor, according to the DALBAR Quantitative Analysis of Investor Behavior, to buy high (because winners bring pleasure) and sell low (so we can avoid even more pain), resulting in sub-par rates of return. What worked for caveman can spell destruction for the 3000 square foot condo man.

Going in, we accept the premise that returns will not be consistent; but we forget it as soon as we suffer a down month, or God forbid, a down year. Rather than logically accept that returns, like life, are never linear, we panic, convincing ourselves that this time the Zombie Apocalypse is real. Then we sell.

Of course, once the zombies fail to appear at our doorstep in search of flesh, we then realize the error of our ways and start investing again...after the market has recovered.

In addition to fighting the natural tendencies of our brain, we are bombarded with messages from the media who are well aware that fear sells newspapers and TV commercials.

A second major threat that requires rescue is taxation. Unlike past generations, Baby Boomers and beyond must deal with the intricacies of having their retirement savings in accounts like 401k's, 403b's, and IRA's. Most, if not all, of these accounts have never been taxed. The piper is paid at retirement. But what if taxes rise in the future to finance our ever increasing national debt?

Other threats facing today's and tomorrow's retiree include Social Security (when do I take it; how will it be taxed) and long term healthcare.

So is the individual investor simply doomed to fail? Not at all. Steps can be taken to put the odds for success in your favor, but you must first understand what you may not know. Let's begin.

--Dan Cuprill & Nikki Earley

Lesson Number One: There is No Nostradamus

"Uncertainty is the only certainty there is, and knowing how to live with insecurity is the only security." --John Allen Paulos

Imagine a TV network dedicated to fortune telling. Every day, it features highly educated people who strongly believe they can predict the future. Like Isaiah, they offer their prophecy for free. Unlike Isaiah, these seers are wrong about 80% of the time. Yet, despite the failures, viewers continue to watch. Even worse, many stake their entire personal fortunes on the advice.

Would you watch such a network? Millions do. In fact, there isn't just one such channel, but two: Fox Business Channel and CNBC.

Go ahead...turn them on, especially around noon on a weekday. These channels bring on one market "expert" after another to give out stock tips or some insight as to where the market is headed.

Here's a little reality: No one...and we mean no one...knows where investment markets are headed in the next week, month, or year. If they did know, they certainly wouldn't tell you for free. In fact, they wouldn't tell you at all because such information would be far too valuable to even sell.

Remember the rule of transitive properties from Mrs. Cheeseman's math class (more on her in a minute). If A is greater than B...and B is greater than C, then A is also greater than C. Or to put it another way, if Bill is taller than Mike, and Mike is taller than Jim, then Bill is also taller than Jim. Got it?

Okay...now pay very close attention.

Markets react to news. Do you agree? Every time stocks drop in price, isn't there always some news event attributed to it (9/11, Microsoft anti-trust suit, the Fed raising interest rates, earnings reports lower than expected)?

News is unpredictable. Do you agree? Did you know any of the following events would happen before they actually occurred?

1. Hijacked airplanes crashing into the World Trade Center and the Pentagon.
2. The Kennedy Assassination.
3. The announcement of Toxic Asset Relief Program.
4. Arthur Anderson's false accounting of Enron.
5. Pearl Harbor (okay...this one isn't fair. You probably weren't alive).

In response to each of these news events, equity markets dropped rapidly. If you did know about these events a week before they actually occurred, you could have made billions of dollars.

Two movies come to mind that demonstrate this reality.

<u>Casino Royale (2006)</u>: James Bond seeks to defeat a card playing terrorist who makes huge rates of return by shorting stocks on companies and then staging acts of sabotage on those corporations because he knows it will drive down their stock price. In other words, he knows the news before anyone else because he's creating it.

<u>Wall Street (1987)</u>: Gordon Gekko hires aspiring trader Bud Fox to "stop sending me information and start bringing me some." So, Bud breaks into offices at night, spies on company executives, and relays insider information told to him by his father. As a result, Gekko has "news" that no one else

has, allowing him to trade ahead of the market.

So, if news is unpredictable and market performance reacts to news, then market performance is unpredictable.

Wait a minute. Are you saying then that all those Wall Street experts like Jim Cramer and Charles Paine really have no idea what they're talking about?

Yes...and No. They certainly know many things. But so do millions of other traders. Everything they know is already factored into a stock's price. It's what they don't know, the future news, which will drive stock prices. They are simply speculating as to what they think the news will be.

Sometimes they get it right...most of the time they get it wrong. Studies show that on average 80% of all professional portfolio managers fail to beat their benchmark index. Of the 20% who do, there are very few repeaters.

The Law of Large Numbers

Imagine we fill the New Orleans Super Dome with 35,000 people. On the PA system, we instruct them all to stand up and remove a quarter from their pocket.

On our mark, they all flip the coin. Those who flipped heads (about 17,500) remain standing. Those who flipped tails sit down. We now repeat this exercise, again and again. With 35,000 people flipping coins, we are willing to bet our houses that at least one person in the dome will flip heads ten straight times. In fact, we wouldn't be surprised if at least 20 people did it.

The law of large numbers states that if you have enough people try to do something, someone will succeed regardless of skill level. The individual who tossed heads 10 straight times...is he an expert coin flipper? Does he somehow understand the gravitational properties between his quarter, his wrist, and the earth? Or was he just lucky?

Guess how many professional portfolio managers exist today? Yup...about 35,000. Over 2,000 work for Fidelity alone. Someone is bound to speculate correctly on the market's reaction to news that has yet to occur.

The successful coin flipper is called lucky. The successful stock picker is called a guru and gets his face on magazines.

Again, we'll concede that these people are smart. Most went to the very best business schools in the country where they were taught that markets and stock prices are not predictable. But when they arrived on Wall Street, they were told how their firms really make money: trades.

Over 1 billion trades a month at $9 per trade on the New York Stock Exchange alone. You do the math. It is in *their* best interest to trade...not yours.

We do think that these very smart people honestly believe they have found a peek into the future. If there were only a handful of them researching companies, then they might actually be onto something. But there are thousands, all crunching the same data. Furthermore, their efforts to buy and sell ahead of the market incur costs that lower their rates of return.

In 2013, Eugene Fama won the Nobel Prize in economics for stating in the 1960's that something is worth only what someone is willing to pay for it. Called The Efficient Market Hypothesis, Fama showed (with a bunch of math) that the current price of stock or bond is the correct price. Nothing is overvalued or undervalued until someone offers or agrees to a different price.

If you buy a house for $300,000, spend $50,000 for improvement, and put it up for sale, how much is it worth if the highest offer you receive is $290,000?

Correct. It's worth $290,000.

So if it's true for real estate, why not stocks?

The $6 watch

Zach Norris is a young man with a passion for fine watches. Understanding that often people don't know the value of their old jewelry, he routinely visits thrift shops and garage sales looking for great deals. If he sees a watch that he knows he can quickly resell for a profit, he will buy it for the asking price and then quickly find a new buyer. In January of 2015, he bought a $6 watch at his local Goodwill store and then sold it for $35,000.

Norris is to watches what Wall Street portfolio managers aspire to be to stocks. But unlike Mr. Norris, they deal in public information. Had Goodwill known the watch was worth $35,000, would they have sold it for $6? Or, would the prior owner have given away the watch to Goodwill in the first place? Of course not. Mr. Norris had insider knowledge. In this case, he can legally act on it. But in the world of security trading, such a move can land you in jail (see Martha Stewart and Bud Fox).

Perhaps there was a time when news traveled slowly enough for someone to get a jump. Those days are over.

There is no Nostradamus. News occurs randomly, and so too will stock and bond prices. All we have going for us is that over the history of mankind, good news has outperformed bad. Despite world wars, famines, epidemics, assassinations, national debt, and disco, capitalism finds a way to improve the quality of life. The quality of your life today dwarfs that of every king and queen of the middle ages. It dwarfs that of your great grandparents, and even your grandparents. Is it not only logical to assume that in the future we will witness massive amounts of bad news but overall, we will prosper?

We don't need Nostradamus to conclude that optimistically is the realistic way to view the future. Hence, actions like market timing and stock picking are far less likely to succeed than buying, holding, and rebalancing a broadly diversified portfolio.

Don't just take our word for it (books to read)

The Investment Answer by Daniel Goldie and Gordon Murray

Random Walk Down Wall Street by Burton Malkeil

The Smartest Investment Book You'll Ever Own by Dan Solin

What Wall Street Doesn't Want You to Know by Larry Swedroe

Winning the Loser's Game by Charles Ellis

Lesson Two: Mrs. Cheeseman Will Rise Again

"Mathematics are well and good but nature keeps dragging us around by the nose. " –
Albert Einstein

You remember Mrs. Cheeseman...the matronly math teacher who has been teaching out of the same book for thirty years because "the math hasn't changed. As you looked at the inside cover of the book, you saw the names and years of the prior holders. "Was it as boring for Fred Saddlemire in 1968 as it is for me now?" you asked yourself. "Was Mrs. Cheeseman ever cool?"

The one question that rose above all others was, "Will I ever need to know this stuff?"

Mrs. Cheeseman assured us we would. Now you're about to see at she was right.

Meet Hans & Franz. When not pumping iron and injecting themselves with steroids, they are drawing income from their savings accumulated from years on late night TV. Aside from an occasional State Farm commercial, the two are pretty much retired.

Convinced that no one should invest like a girlie man, Hans has invested heavily in equities under the belief that over time he stands to earn a higher rate of return. Chances are he'll be right.

Franz is no stranger to machismo, but opts for a portfolio that is likely to produce a lower, more consistent rate of return. Starting with one million each, they both desire to withdraw $50,000 per year to supplement their SNL royalty checks.

Hans and Franz are about to learn what Mrs. Cheeseman taught us years ago.

Average may not be as important as consistency of return.

Hans: $1,000,000			
Year	Withdrawal	Return	Y/E Value
1	$50,000.00	-13	$826,500.00
2	$50,000.00	-20%	$661,200.00
3	$50,000.00	5%	$694,260.00
4	$50,000.00	-7%	$599,161.80
5	$50,000.00	20%	$658,994.16
6	$50,000.00	25%	$761,242.70
7	$50,000.00	-25%	$533,432.03
8	$50,000.00	45%	$700,976.44
9	$50,000.00	30%	$846,269.37
10	$50,000.00	20%	***$908,060.56***
Return Average: 8%			

Franz: $1,000,000			
Year	Withdrawal	Return	Y/E Value
1	$50,000.00	6%	$1,007,000.00
2	$50,000.00	8%	$1,087,560.00
3	$50,000.00	7%	$1,163,689.20
4	$50,000.00	11%	$1,236,195.01
5	$50,000.00	-4%	$1,138,747.21
6	$50,000.00	6%	$1,154,072.04
7	$50,000.00	12%	$1,236,560.69
8	$50,000.00	-2%	$1,162,829.48
9	$50,000.00	10%	$1,224,112.42
10	$50,000.00	6%	***$1,244,559.17***
Return Average: 6%			

As you can see, although Hans indeed earned a higher average return (8% vs. 6%) at the end of ten years, he has considerably less money than his body-building brother. Why? Every year, the two sell a part of their portfolios' shares to generate cash. When shares rise in value, it requires fewer shares to generate $50,000. When share prices fall, Hans must sell more. Those extra shares, once sold, are gone. It matters not what his portfolio does in the future in relation to those shares. He will never get them back

By minimizing his potential downside, Franz has more money even though he averaged less over time. Fewer negative years means he sells fewer shares.

This phenomenon exists only because Hans and Franz need to sell shares for cash. Had they never needed to sell shares, then Hans would have more much money than Franz, despite the volatility. This is the Math of Retirement.

Mrs. Cheeseman taught us that nothing in life performs consistently--not the weather, not your golf score, and certainly not an investment portfolio. This lack of consistency can be measured. It is called standard deviation. The lower the standard deviation, the more likely you will earn the average return each and every year. So, if you found a portfolio with a guaranteed return of 8% every year, then the standard deviation would be zero. Good luck finding that. Chances are, the best you'll do in seeking your 8% is a portfolio with a standard deviation of ten. So, what does that mean?

If Average Return is 8% and Standard Deviation is ten, then:

66% of the time: You will have a one year return between -2% and 18%.

95% of the time: You will have a one year return between -12% and 28%.

99% of the time: You will have a one year return between -22% and 38%.

If you are an investor, then your portfolio also has a long term average return and a standard deviation to go along with it. The problem is that very few people know this, nor do they understand the "normal" volatility that comes with it. If they did, we think they'd be much less likely to panic.

For example, if a portfolio has the dimensions described in the chart above, should we be surprised (or even disappointed) if we earn a return of -6% in a given year?

Of course not. We already know going in that this is very likely. We also know that over time, it's more likely that we'll have more positive results than negative results. Guaranteed? No. Likely? Yes.

Think of it like baking a cake. You can put in the best ingredients, but you have soup unless you put the cake in the oven for the right amount of time.

Results do not come in a linear fashion, no matter how badly we wish they did. What in life does? Do the giant redwoods of northern California grow the same number of feet every year? Does it take you the same number of minutes to drive to work each day? Do farmers dig up their corn seeds every few days to see if they are sprouting, or have they learned to trust the process?

It is essential that you know the long term average return and standard deviation of your portfolio allocation. Without knowing, you are simply winging it; and your survival mechanism stands a much better chance of over-riding your logic.

Know your math. Make Mrs. Cheeseman proud!

Don't just take our word for it (books to read):

The Intelligent Asset Allocator by William Bernstein

All About Asset Allocation by Richard Feri

Asset Allocation by Roger Gibson

Lesson Number Three: The Boogeyman is Real

"The only two things that scare me are God and the IRS" –Dr. Dre

Assuming that you do not define patriotism by the amount you pay in tax, what follows should be useful.

If you're one of the 53% of Americans who pay federal income taxes, then it is likely you pay more than what is legally required. If you own a small business, then it's almost a sure thing that you are over paying.

The Seven Most Expensive Words in the English Language: My CPA takes care of my taxes.

From our experience, most CPAs do a great job of filing taxes; but very few actually do any tax real planning. When I ask people, when was the last time their CPA said he found a way to lower your taxes by $4,000, they usually give me a blank stare and then say, "Never."

Does your CPA/Tax Preparer ever:

- Call you with proactive strategies to achieve a tax free retirement?

- Demonstrate how to restructure your 401k/403b/IRA accounts to avoid future taxation?

- How to collect your social security benefits TAX FREE?

- Show you how to structure your business to minimize employment taxes?

- Show you how to write off your family's medical bills as a business expense?

- Show you how you can hire children (or grandchildren) to shift income from yourself to them?

- Help you choose the right retirement plan for your business?

- Explain how each of your investments is taxed and make suggestions on how to reduce it?

- Advise you on how to carefully consider which investments belong in taxable accounts and which investments belong in tax-advantaged accounts?

- Develop a plan for maximizing the value of any long-term capital loss carryforwards?

- Explain the rules governing "passive" income and losses and have a plan to avoid "suspended" losses?

- Meet with you throughout the year to discuss your business--or does he just wait until taxes are due?

- Give you a plan for minimizing taxes-- or does he/she just wing it every year?

Aside from investing behavior, income taxes are the greatest obstacle to most investors. There is never an age at which you stop paying them. You paid tax on your social security as you put money into the system, and you will likely pay tax on the money as it comes out.

When you reach age 70.5, you must start paying tax on your retirement plans (401k, IRA, 403b). When you die, your heirs must also pay tax on whatever is left.

Your estate may be taxed again for simply being too big.

The code is, by design, very complicated. Too often, people just go along with it, unaware of the steps that can legally reduce their federal and state income taxes. This is especially important during retirement.

You have a choice of paying taxes now...or later. To many, procrastination seems logical when it comes paying the IRS. For years people have socked away massive amounts of money in 401ks, 403bs, IRAs. The idea is you invest it now in a tax deductible account while you're in a high tax bracket. Then you withdraw it at a lower tax bracket when you retire. Or so you hope.

What if taxes rise in the future? Our country, as of 2016, owes close to $20 trillion. Projections suggest this amount will continue to rise as more and more baby boomers retire. Fewer people paying taxes and more requiring things like Medicare, Medicaid, and Social Security.

Case Study

Bill & Karen Tucker are both 65. Retired, they each have a rollover IRA worth $600,000. Bill collects $2,200 a month from social security. Karen receives $1,800. They need $7,000 a month to live comfortably, so they withdraw $3,000 a month from their retirement accounts. To determine how much of their social security check is subject to taxation, we add the IRA withdrawals ($36,000) to one-half of the social security payments ($24,000) This gives them a modified adjust gross income (MAGI) of $60,000. Whenever the MAGI exceeds $44,000 for a married couple, then up to 85% of their check is subjected to taxation.

Assuming they file jointly and use the standard deduction, Bill & Karen owe $4,300 in Federal income taxes. Now, what if they had decided a few years back to convert their rollover IRAs to a Roth IRA? Doing so would have triggered at the time of conversion, but no tax would ever be owned on the accounts again. Even if their accounts double in value, there is no tax associated with a Roth withdrawal. Not only is there no tax on Roth IRA withdrawals, but now there would also be no tax owed on their Social Security benefits. Furthermore, Bill & Karen could now withdraw an additional $16,400 from their taxable IRA and still pay $0 in tax since they still have their standard deduction and exemption to apply.

Imagine if federal income tax rates double in the future. By converting to a Roth, the Tucker's have protected themselves.

Another tax advantaged vehicle is permanent life insurance. Money in the policy grows tax deferred and can be accessed tax free via a policy loan. While I don't usually recommend retirees buy life insurance, this feature is a great reason to keep your policy even after you've stopped working.

Like a lot of people we meet, the Tuckers rely solely on their accountant for tax advice. But from our experience, many accountants work as tax filers, not tax planners.

Tax planning is one of the most ignored areas of financial planning, and failure to address IRS lien on savings is ruining people. It is not the job of the IRS to tell you how to lower your taxes. It's your job. If you don't know how, you need to find a professional who does. You won't find him inside a box of turbo tax software.

The tax code is very complicated. Too often people just go along with it, unaware of the steps that can legally reduce their federal and state income taxes. Failure to address this issue can mean you're not worth anywhere close to what you think.

If you want to know more about real tax planning, call us at 513-563-PLAN (7526). We'll show you how we use our Tax Blueprint™ to rescue retirement plans for our clients.

Don't just take our word for it (books to read):

How to Pay Zero Taxes 2016 by J.K. Lasser

The Power of Zero by David McKnight

Lesson Number Four: It will probably end badly

"It's paradoxical, that the idea of living a long life appeals to everyone, but the idea of getting old doesn't appeal to anyone." – Andy Rooney

The first chapter ended with a statement that the future is always likely to be better than the past. For society as a whole, we truly believe that. As for our individual lives, we know that life is finite. The Grim Reaper is undefeated. And while modern medicine has made huge strides in fighting heart disease, diabetes, and cancer, we all still die.

The lucky ones will die suddenly, like Tim Russert. Here today living life to the fullest...gone tomorrow. Sad for our loved ones, but much better than dying a slow death where our health declines daily, limited to a wheelchair, incapable of recalling our children's names, and needing assistance to visit the bathroom.

Depressing...isn't it? That's life.

As a society, we are living longer. That is a good thing, but that also means our money must last longer. It means that eventually we will become weak and likely to need help with those things we only want to do for ourselves (custodial care).

Some stats from the National Institute for Health:

- If you reach age 65, there's a 70% chance you'll need custodial care.
- The average nursing home stay is almost three years.
- The average nursing home cost is $70,000 a year.
- Nursing home costs rise at twice the average inflation rate.

- Medicare doesn't pay for Long Term Care.
- Medicaid is available only after you've spent down your assets.
- Most people in nursing homes are on Medicaid, but they didn't start there.

Basically, you have three options when it comes to long term care.

- First, you can self-insure the exposure. Perhaps you have enough money to do just that. Remember...it's $70,000 a year now. At 6% inflation, the price will double in twelve years. If you're married and you get sick, will that leave enough money for your healthy spouse?

- Second, you can rely on Medicaid. Why not? Most do, but, that's available only after you've spent down your own money. If you're married, Medicaid kicks in when you have about $100,000 left. You don't have to sell your house, but the government may attach a lien to it after you die so that it can recoup the cost of your care.

- Third, you can buy long term care insurance. For many people, this is the right choice. Often we hear people say they won't buy it out of fear they'll never use it, and thus waste their money. We're going to let you in on a little secret: the people who go to nursing homes with long term care don't win the game. It's those who have long term care insurance but die peacefully in their sleep, healthy today...dead tomorrow, who win the game.

When your car isn't stolen, do you regret owing auto insurance? Never feel regret for being prudent.

Long term care insurance can be expensive, but a few things can be done to reduce it:

1. Limit coverage to four years. Odds are very high you won't need the policy after four years. By limiting coverage to four years, you reduce the cost dramatically over a lifetime benefit policy.

2. Self-insure a part of the cost. If nursing homes in your area cost $200 per day, consider coverage for $150. Be sure to study the long term impact of not being fully insured.

3. Ask your children to pay for it. They are the ones who stand to benefit

from you not spending all of their inheritance on nursing home care.

Whatever you do...have a plan! It's not a matter of if, but when!

Don't just take our word for it:

Long Term Care: <u>Your Financial Planning Guide</u> by Phyllis Shelton

---

Lesson Number Five: Your Brain is Messed Up

"We have seen the enemy, and he is us."—Pogo

Perhaps the biggest obstacle (no, not *perhaps*...it really *is* the biggest) toward financial success is our own brain...our humanness...our emotions.

God gave us many gifts; but if misused, they can be self-destructive.

Consider weight loss. Technically, losing weight is very easy. We simply exercise more and eat less. Yet, we are the fattest nation on earth; and weight loss is a multi-billion dollar industry. Why?

Investing is also quite simple: buy when prices are low. Sell when they are high.

According to the Dalbar study, we see that simple strategy ignored all the time. People often do the complete opposite.

Let's take Marty McFly's time traveling Delorean back a few years....to 10,000 BC.

Meet your great, great, great, great, great, great, great, great, great (you get the idea) grandfather. We'll call him Fred. He lives in a cave with his mate Wilma and their children Pebbles and Bam Bam (whom they adopted after a T-Rex ate Barney & Betty Rubble).

Life is very simple for Fred and Wilma. Fred wakes up, sharpens his spear, and kills whatever he can find. He brings it back to the cave where Wilma cooks it.

Fred is motivated to stop the pains of hunger, cold, and predators. He seeks warmth and comfort where he can; but above all else, he tries to avoid pain for his family and himself. He doesn't know it, but Fred has within his brain a survival mechanism that motivates him to behave this way. It is his natural tendency to flee from danger. In fact, all animals have it-- another gift from God. Fred doesn't worry about his cholesterol level, his A1C results, or his blood pressure. He merely wants to stay fed, warm, and safe. Fred was the original couch potato whenever the opportunity presented itself.

Food, water, safety, and warmth...that's all he thinks about. Morality, personal fulfillment, spirituality....these don't matter to him at all. It's a struggle just to meet the basics.

Fast forward to present day. We don't have Fred's worries. Far from it. Food? In the US, a major health problem amongst our poor is obesity. Water, warmth...readily available. The survival mechanism that kept Fred alive until a sabretooth tiger ate him is still present in our brains. We don't use it often, but it's there...lurking.

Need to lose weight by eating less (painful) and exercising (even more painful). Forget it. Our brain tells us we're crazy. Stay in bed. Rest. Relax.

Fred didn't care if he lived past age 40, but you do. Rather than helping you though, the survival mechanism is betraying you.

When your stocks fall in value, you experience pain. Your brain tells you that you must do something. You must sell. When what you sold starts increasing in value, you feel worse! You know logically that stocks are likely to rebound, but your brain convinces you that "this time is different."

While the survival mechanism is the worse feature of our psyche when it comes to investing, there are a few others that can be equally destructive:

Herding: When we were teenaged, we called it "peer pressure". Our mothers asked, "If Johnny told you to jump off a bridge, would you?" Hey, bridge jumping can be great fun.

When Frank in accounting tells you that everyone is dumping the index fund in the company 401k and loading up heavily on company stock, you need to remind yourself of something. Unless Frank is having secret meetings with the company chairman, he knows nothing more than the rest of the world. All the information about your company is already factored into its stock. Frank is just speculating. Sadly, there were several "Franks" working at Enron.

Confirmation Bias: We'd all like to believe that we are objective thinkers, weighing all facts before making a decision or establishing a belief. Sorry...not true. There are things we WANT to believe are true. So much so, we'll ignore any evidence to the contrary. Take Nikki's daughter, Georgie. At age 8, she is committed to believing in Santa Clause. She's heard from classmates that St. Nick isn't real, but every year she finds evidence to the contrary (thanks to her mom). In her mind, the kids who don't believe are simply the ones who misbehave and receive nothing on December 25th.

For other people, we see confirmation bias in areas like climate change, the Kennedy assassination, or the future price of gold.

In 2001, Dan met a GE engineer who said he had no intention of ever diversifying away from his company stock. "I don't want to hear it," he said to us when we suggested a broader allocation. He was 64, and the stock comprised 100% of his portfolio. In the previous ten years, his net worth had tripled. It seemed invincible.

At that point, the stock was trading at $65 a share. Seven years later, it was worth $8.

When it comes to matters of finance, confirmation bias can be expensive.

Gambler's Fallacy: The roulette wheel has come up red the last six times. It must turn up black this time, right? No wait...six times in a row? It has to turn up red a seventh time. It's on a roll.

Of course, both statements are false. The Gambler believes that despite randomness, past events influence further events. This is why casinos give free hotel rooms to high rollers. Just don't leave our casino. We know eventually you will give the money back. You'll believe you have skill, but we know it is pure chance...and the odds of chance favor the house.

We see it with stocks all the time. The market is up, and "experts" call for a "correction". In order for there to be a correction, we must first have a mistake. The "correction assumption" is that stocks are mispriced. Eventually the market will wake up this reality, causing prices to adjust.

It's hogwash. News drives stock prices. Markets will move randomly because news occurs randomly.

Anchoring: Back to our GE engineer. His wife saw the potential mistake of holding just one stock, but even she couldn't be swayed toward logic because they knew diversification would trigger taxation. So anchored was she in her belief that taxes are bad, she put herself in a position of eventually owing no tax because they lost most of their portfolio in 2008. Oh, to have Marty's Delorean.

A successful investor understands that logic doesn't come naturally. He seeks out ways to ensure that when it comes to money, the left side of his brain stays in control.

Don't just take our word for it (books to read):

Predictably Irrational by Dan Ariely

The Behavior Gap by Carl Richards

Lesson Number Six: Rick Perry was right.

"The real sin with Social Security is that it's a long-term rip-off and a short-term scam."—Tony Snow

A Ponzi scheme is an investment fraud that involves the payment of purported returns to existing investors from funds contributed by new investors. Ponzi scheme organizers often solicit new investors by promising to invest funds in opportunities claimed to generate high returns with little or no risk. In many Ponzi schemes, the fraudsters focus on attracting new money to make promised payments to earlier-stage investors to create the false appearance that investors are profiting from a legitimate business.

With little or no legitimate earnings, Ponzi schemes require a consistent flow of money from new investors to continue. Ponzi schemes tend to collapse when it becomes difficult to recruit new investors or when a large number of investors ask to cash out.

--United States Securities & Exchange Commission

In the 2012 election primary, pundits attacked Texas Governor Rick Perry for correctly describing the Social Security system as a Ponzi scheme. The system, which began in 1937, then taxed 37 workers for every retiree a maximum total of $30 per year. Today, it taxes three workers for every retiree 6.2% of their earnings (up to $118,550). If you're self-employed, you pay the tax twice.

Money is taken from workers and is transferred to retirees. The rate of return is not guaranteed. Most people will average between two and four percent. Many will lose money if they die before they receive benefits equal to their contributions. Unlike your savings, you cannot leave your social security benefits to your children. At least Charles Ponzi gave some investors a high rate of return.

Social Security today is not what it was intended to be when President Roosevelt signed the program into existence in 1935.

Its original intent was to aid Americans who couldn't take care of themselves, such as widows and orphans. It was never designed to be the sole means for retirement income, which it has become for many Americans today.

In 1935, life expectancy was 58; while the earliest one could collect benefits back then was age 65. On average, you were more likely to die than receive benefits. Ironically, the very first person to receive a check, Ida May Fuller, lived to be 100 years old. These days about 58 million people receive benefits.

Benefit Timing

For many retirees, the question of when to take benefits can be a difficult one. The longer you wait to start collecting, the larger your monthly check. Full retirement age is between 62 and 67 depending on what year you were born.

You can take benefits as early as 62, but receive 25% less per month than if you hold out until your full retirement age. If you wait until age 70 to collect, then you get 32% more. In real dollars that means if your full retirement benefit is $2,000 but you elected to take it at 62, you will receive $1,500 each month. Likewise, if you wait until age 70, you will receive $2,700 every month.

Life expectancy plays a major role in determining the timing of your social security benefits. The breakeven point for taking benefits at 62 vs. 70 is age 78.

If you had that time machine and knew your expiration date – no problem. Of course if you delay taking your benefit, it may mean you have to spend more of your savings in the early years of retirement.

Many factors need to be taken into consideration when taking social security.

For a free Social Security timing report, visit our website, www.matsonandcuprill.com.

So what is the future of Social Security? Is it sustainable? What was once a 1% tax is now 6.2%. As fewer people pay in and more are recipients, the percentage could always be increased. The amount of income subject to the tax could be increased, and inflationary increases could be eliminated or decreased. Lots of appealing options...

No political party wants to broach the elimination of Social Security, and they likely won't. Social Security in its current state isn't at all what Roosevelt had in mind in 1935, so change is always a strong possibility.

Don't Just Take Our Word For It:

 Get What's Yours: The Secrets to Maxing Out Your Social Security by Laurence J. Kotlikoff, Phillip Moeller and Paul Solman

Number Seven: Flat Abs, a low A1C, and Wealth: To get these, you probably need help

"Everyone needs a coach. It doesn't matter whether you're a basketball player, a tennis player, a gymnast or a bridge player." --Bill Gates

At age 51, he finally got the news: "Dan, you're fat, your blood sugar is too high, and so is your blood pressure. Other than that, you're doing great...for a 70 year old."

He couldn't argue with the doctor. Everything he said was true.

"If you're serious about this, I can coach you through it," he said. "Every three months, going forward, you'll come in for new blood work and a review of your eating habits for the past three months. In addition, you'll spend time with my nutritionist. Lastly, you will hire a personal trainer who will give you a full body workout three times a week."

Three months later, Dan lost 15 pounds, and my blood sugar level (A1C) dropped from 7.1 to 5.7 (you want it below 6.5).

Could he have done it without the nutritionist and trainer? Technically, yes. Realistically, not a chance. When the alarm goes off at 5:30 a.m., he now jumps out of bed because the trainer awaits him at the gym. If it were up to Dan to work out alone, that alarm would never be set. He admits he would just procrastinate. When he did get around to exercising, it would be with half the intensity his trainer demands. Why? Because exercise is painful. Sleep is pleasurable. Steel cut oatmeal doesn't taste nearly as good as a Dunkin' Donut.

On our own, we rarely perform at our optimal level. A good coach will not only help achieve excellence, he'll assist in keeping us there. A good coach sees things we can't (or don't want to see). He forces us to leave our comfort zone and to apply logic when emotion is in overdrive. He holds us accountable to ourselves.

One of the biggest failings in the financial services industry is the failure to understand this. The industry is dominated not by coaches (or even advisors) but by commission salesmen. They push product as the answer and then go looking for the question. Objectivity is lost, and the client pays the price.

A good wealth coach services his client with a holistic approach and commits himself to putting the needs of the client first.

Over 20 years, we've refined our process to offer such a service. It's a four step process called The Wealth Coaching Program.

Step One: The Consultation-- We begin every first meeting with a simple question: "What will make this a great meeting for you today?" We want the client to set the agenda. More importantly, we want to know what keeps them up at night.

If on a scale of one to ten (ten means you sleep like Bill Gates, and one means you don't sleep at all), how do you rate your financial situation? If you are a nine or a ten, you're done. Give this book to a friend, and go live your life. No need for any coaching. You are Tiger Woods in 2000.

But if you are more like a seven (or lower), then what has to occur for you to be a ten, aside from winning the lottery? We find that it's rarely about the amount of money one has. The most anxious people we've ever met had significant wealth. Despite that, they were fearful, frustrated, and even angry. In some cases, they were victimized by other advisors. To get most people to a ten, it takes a strategy that they have a hand in designing. They require a plan that details fully the pros and cons, and is simple enough that they can explain it to a friend.

Do you need to be a financial expert to be a ten? No. Just like we don't need to know how a hybrid engine works to drive a car. We do need to know how to start the car (which if you haven't bought a car lately, isn't as easy as it used to be). We need to know how to put the car in gear, and how to turn the wheel. We need to know when gas is needed, when to rotate the tires, and when to change the oil. Simple stuff, but it is required.

A well designed financial strategy answers questions like:

1. How much can I spend during retirement without a strong chance of going broke?

2. What rate of return do I really need on my money, and how can I get it with the least amount of volatility?

3. How can I protect myself from speculation (stock picking, market timing)?

4. How will I deal with catastrophe, such as failing health?

5. How can I legally pay the IRS less?

6. How can I most efficiently transfer my assets at death?

Step Two: The Creation-- Then questions to step one are answered by making you part of the plan's design. A good coach listens to what you want to accomplish (I want $X a month for life, after tax, indexed for inflation) and then offers the pros and cons of achieving that goal. And trust me...there are always cons. Lots of them. You need to know them.

Together we draw up the plan. How much of your income do you want guaranteed? Before you say "all of it," know that guaranteed usually comes with two costs: low return and less for your heirs.

If you choose to have some or all of your money in a non-guaranteed portfolio, do you fully understand the likely range of returns? What is your worst year likely to

P a g e |**65**

be (statistically)? And when it happens (and it will), what will you do?

How much (if any) would you like to leave your children?

How do you wish to handle the cost of custodial care should you need it (and you probably will)?

If you choose to make no changes, what are your chances for success? Are you okay with that?

Step Three: The Consideration--Only after the design is fully complete can the plan be written. Back when Dan's blood results showed he had too much sugar in his blood, he and his doctor together discussed the ups and downs of the strategy: costs, time, denial of certain foods, etc. Once that was outlined, then they actually created a written plan.

Medications can be used to fight illness. The doctor doesn't care where you fill the prescription. He simply wants you to fully take the meds.

In personal finance, products are the medication. While a coach can assist you in acquiring them, it should not be a requirement for being coached. Sadly, we too often see financial advisors offer "free" planning. There is no such thing as free. You will pay for it, one way or another. Typically, the "plan" is nothing more than a sales proposal to buy product. "We'll give you a free plan that will recommend you buy a commission-based product from us."

In addition delivering the written plan, we provide the client with a list of recommendations on a single page. With each recommendation, we ask a few simple questions:

1. Do you fully understand this recommendation? Do you know the pros and cons?

2. Are you going to implement it (yes or no…never a "let me think about it")?

3. How are you going to implement it? Are you going work with someone (insurance agent, investment advisor)?

No loose ends.

Step Four: The Coaching & Education Stage-- Our firm educates our clients in groups, but coaches them one on one. Some of the education classes many times reiterate important concepts that are helpful in understanding the long term issues facing retirement. Other classes delve deeper into the client's emotions. Almost all of our decisions are emotion based. We need to accept and understand that. By being in tune with our values, we are much more likely to reach a purpose for our money that reflects these values.

Our Offer to You

Although not nearly as complicated as many make it out to be, personal finance does have enough complexity that it can not only lead some to make mistakes, but also scare others to the point where they do very little in retirement out of fear they will go broke before they die.

Few things are more tragic than being filled with regret on one's death bed, especially if those regrets were avoidable. For many, it's a matter of getting the right amount of help.

If you do plan on working with a professional, we've outlined below some suggestions:

1. Begin the relationship with a written plan. Work only with someone who charges you for it. People who give

away advice for free have an ulterior motive, and it's not to offer you objective advice.

2. Ask the advisor to explain his world view on investments. Does he believe that markets are predictable or not? Be sure that his opinion matches yours.

3. Credentials do matter. As a recent commercial demonstrated, anyone can call themselves a financial advisor. We suggest working with one who is a Certified Financial Planner. This won't make him/her perfect, but it will at least speak to the education he or she has obtained in the field.

4. Check to see if he or she has ever been reprimanded by FINRA or the SEC.

5. Go with your gut. Dan's wife could never logically explain to her parents why she married him. Thirty years later, it seems her gut was right. Trust cannot be explained logically. It's a feeling. If your gut says "no", then keep looking.

We'd love to share with you our unique planning process, the Wealth Coaching Program. If you call our office to arrange a free consultation, we'll also give you our Retirement Rescue Toolkit. It's loaded with great reports, CD's, and other books that delve into the topics we just shared. Even if you choose not to work with us, the Retirement Rescue Tool Kit is yours to keep.

To learn more about Dan & Nikki's financial coaching services, email them:

- dan@matsonandcuprill.com
- nikki@matsonandcuprill.com

Or visit www.matsonandcuprill.com

513-623-0259

34244122R00042

Made in the USA
San Bernardino, CA
23 May 2016